SPECIAL OPS

PARARESCUE
JUMPERS

LEE SLATER

**Checkerboard
Library**

An Imprint of Abdo Publishing
abdopublishing.com

abdopublishing.com

Published by Abdo Publishing, a division of ABDO, PO Box 398166, Minneapolis, Minnesota 55439.
Copyright © 2016 by Abdo Consulting Group, Inc. International copyrights reserved in all countries.
No part of this book may be reproduced in any form without written permission from the publisher.
Checkerboard Library™ is a trademark and logo of Abdo Publishing.

Printed in the United States of America, North Mankato, Minnesota
102015
012016

Cover Photo: Jonathan Snyder/US Air Force
Interior Photos: Adam Grant/US Air Force, pp. 26–27; Bill Huntington/US Air Force, pp. 5, 28; Cecilio
M. Ricardo Jr./US Air Force, p. 14; Chad Watts/US Air Force, p. 12; Department of Agriculture/Forest
Service/National Archives, p. 28; Dillon Johnston/US Air Force, p. 21; Earl Cooley at Seeley Lake in
1940–KD Swan photo/US Forest Service Collection, p. 8; iStockphoto, p. 23; photo courtesy of Jon
Pearce, p. 11; Rufus Robinson at Moose Creek Ranger Station–US Forest Service Collection, p. 9;
Shutterstock, pp. 4, 6, 8, 10, 12, 14, 18, 20, 22, 23, 24, 26; Steven M. Turner/US Air Force, p. 20;
Tammie Ramsouer/US Air Force, p. 21; US Air Force, pp. 18–19; US Air Force, pp. 6–7, 24, 25, 28; www.
navyseals.com, p. 23

Content Developer: Nancy Tuminelly
Design: Anders Hanson, Mighty Media, Inc.
Editor: Liz Salzmann

Library of Congress Cataloging-in-Publication Data
Slater, Lee, 1969-
 Pararescue jumpers / Lee Slater.
     pages cm. -- (Special ops)
 Includes index.
 ISBN 978-1-62403-972-0
1. United States. Air Force--Parachute troops--Juvenile literature. 2. United States. Air Force--
Search and rescue operations--Juvenile literature. 3. Search and rescue operations--Juvenile
literature. 4. Special forces (Military science)--United States--Juvenile literature. I. Title.
 UG633.S54 2016
 358.4'141--dc23
                        2015026589

CONTENTS

CHAPTER 1

ON THE SCENE DURING
HURRICANE
KATRINA

On August 29, 2005, Hurricane Katrina struck land. The massive storm was 400 miles (644 km) wide. Its winds blew 100 to 140 miles per hour (161 to 225 kmh). The Gulf Coast of the United States was hit hard. The hurricane caused a great deal of damage. But what happened afterward was a catastrophe.

Half of New Orleans, Louisiana, is below sea level. The city is

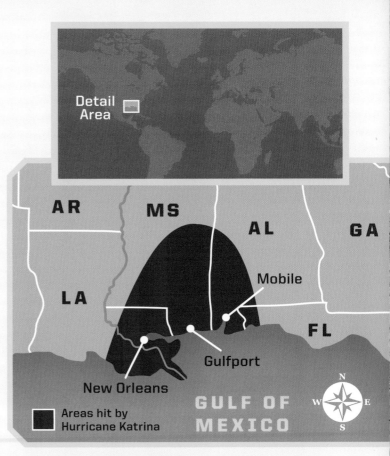

Detail Area

AR   MS   AL   GA

LA   Mobile

FL

Gulfport

New Orleans

GULF OF
MEXICO

■ Areas hit by Hurricane Katrina

Hurricane Katrina did the most damage in Louisiana, Mississippi, Alabama, and Florida.

A Pararescue Jumper looks out of a helicopter over the flooded city of New Orleans.

surrounded by **levees**. The levees keep water from flooding the city. But strong winds and rushing water from Hurricane Katrina broke many of the levees. The water flooded New Orleans. It was worse than anyone in the city had ever seen. Many people were trapped by the flooding and could not get to dry land.

The United States Air Force Pararescue Jumpers were called into action. They used **helicopters** to search for people who were trapped. They rescued people from bridges, rooftops, and flooded buildings.

The Pararescue Jumpers usually rescue military service members who are trapped in enemy territory. But they are just as ready, willing, and able to rescue **civilians**. All together, the Pararescue Jumpers saved more than 4,000 people trapped by Hurricane Katrina.

CHAPTER 2

BEFORE THE PARARESCUE JUMPERS

During **World War I** and **World War II**, military airplanes carried supplies. Airplanes weren't as safe and reliable as they are today. Flying was dangerous and many of the planes went down.

Crashes weren't always deadly for the crew. The pilot might pull off a crash landing. Starting in World War II, the crew, wearing **parachutes**, would sometimes jump out of the plane.

Surviving the crash landing or parachute drop was only the first step. Next, the survivors had to find food, keep warm, and tend to any

injuries. They then had to try to make their way to safety. This was hard to do in cold, remote places such as northern Canada.

Whenever a plane went down, other planes would be sent to search for it. The pilots hoped to find survivors and rescue them. However, even when survivors were located, it could be extremely difficult to get to them. Rescue planes needed clear, even ground to land.

After landing, it might take rescue parties several days to reach the survivors. For someone who was hurt, hungry, and freezing, that could be too long to wait. Today, instead of trying to land a rescue plane, Pararescue Jumpers use **parachutes** to reach stranded or trapped people.

More than 3,000 C-46 airplanes flew supplies during World War II.

A
GAME
CHANGER

To effectively rescue survivors, it is important that Pararescue Jumpers land **accurately**. However, this was not possible before 1940. **Parachutes**

Earl Cooley

at that time were simple, round **parachutes**. Jumpers couldn't steer them.

Then, on July 12, 1940, two US Forest Service smoke jumpers made history. Rufus Robinson and Earl Cooley used steerable parachutes to land in a pinpointed location. This breakthrough made a huge difference to the military. Now they could save time reaching people who needed to be rescued.

Rufus Robinson

The Forest Service firefighters also used special tools to test wind speed and direction. They had skills and equipment for jumping in any weather. Their knowledge was very helpful to the military parachutists.

CHAPTER 4

BLACKIE'S
GANG

During **World War II**, American planes passed from India over Burma to China. This route was called The Hump. The Hump took pilots over the Himalayan mountains and miles of **uncharted** jungle. The few people who lived in the remote area were hostile.

Detail Area

Yarlung Tsangpo River

Dinjan

INDIA

Brahmaputra River

BURMA

CHINA

AIRLIFT TO CHINA (The Hump)

Burma Road

Runming

N
W E
S

Sometimes a plane would not make it over The Hump. After a crash, the plane's crew faced many dangers. These included headhunters and enemy soldiers. The military had no unit that could save the survivors.

Captain John L. "Blackie" Porter

In August 1943, a military plane crashed in northern Burma. The plane was carrying 21 passengers. All but one **parachuted** safely to the ground. The survivors were stranded in the jungle. They were days away from any road. Some of them were injured.

Captain John L. "Blackie" Porter and his crew found the survivors. They dropped food, medical supplies, and weapons. Two **medics** and a surgeon parachuted to the site to care for the injured. They were able to survive until a ground team could reach them. The group was able to walk out together.

Captain Porter's team became known as "Blackie's Gang." Porter was chosen to lead a new search and rescue organization. It was the beginning of what would become the US Air Force Pararescue branch.

CHAPTER 5

PARARESCUE
IS BORN

The US Air Force recognized the need for a highly trained rescue team. The team would use **parachutes** and other means to get to remote places. People who needed to be rescued were often injured or trapped. The rescue team would need medical training too.

The air force officially started the Pararescue branch on July 1, 1947. Every Pararescue team had one doctor and four **technicians**.

PJs practice loading an injured person into a helicopter.

The men were trained experts at **parachuting**, medicine, combat, and survival. The new Pararescuers were sent all over the world on lifesaving missions.

Pararescuers are also known as PJs, which is short for Pararescue Jumpers. Today, there are more than 500 active PJs. They are ready to take on any mission, anytime, anywhere to save lives.

PJs provide emergency medical treatment and rescue services to military **personnel** and **civilians**. They save lives in both combat and peacetime situations. They often perform missions in hostile territory and put themselves in danger. **Intense** Pararescue training prepares the PJs to deal with any kind of emergency.

THE PARARESCUE CREED

"It is my duty as a Pararescueman to save life and to aid the injured. I will be prepared at all times to perform my assigned duties quickly and efficiently, placing these duties before personal desires and comforts. These things I do, that others may live."

CHAPTER 6

THE
PIPELINE

The training program for PJs is called the pipeline. It is one of the most extreme training programs in the American military. It takes between one and two years to complete the pipeline. By the end, 90 percent of the candidates will have dropped out. The few who graduate will serve as the most qualified rescue **specialists** in the world.

Trainees tread water using only their legs. They have 16-pound (7 kg) weights on their belts.

REQUIREMENTS FOR PARARESCUE TRAINING

- male
- joined the US Air Force before 28th birthday
- 20/20 vision (or corrected to 20/20 with glasses)
- not **color-blind**
- passed a flight physical
- between 5 feet and 6 feet 8 inches (152 and 203 cm) tall
- weighs 250 pounds (113 kg) or less
- able to obtain a Secret Security clearance
- US citizen upon start of training
- passed the Physical Abilities and Stamina Test (PAST)

TRAIN LIKE A PJ

Before starting Pararescue training, a candidate has to pass a test of physical **endurance**. Some men train for months to meet the **minimum** standards. It's not at all easy!

Pararescue Physical Ability and Stamina Test (PAST) Standards

PAST EVENT	MINIMUM STANDARDS	OPTIMUM STANDARDS
50-meter underwater swim	pass/fail (no time limit)	
500-meter swim	10 minutes and 7 seconds	9 minutes or less
1.5 Mile Run	9 minutes and 47 seconds	9 minutes or less
Pull-ups (1 minute)	10	20
Sit-ups (2 minutes)	58	100
Pushups (2 minutes)	54	100

PIPELINE COURSES

1. Air Force Basic Military Training

The training that everyone entering the US Air Force goes through.

3. Pararescue/Combat Control Indoctrination Course

This course provides extensive physical conditioning. It also includes dive training, medical training, history, and leadership training.

5. Air Force Underwater Egress Training

Training in how to escape from an aircraft that has landed in the water.

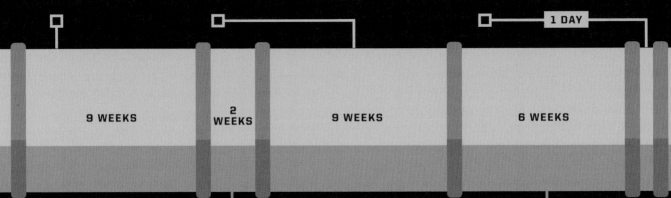

1 DAY

9 WEEKS

2 WEEKS

9 WEEKS

6 WEEKS

After completing all of these courses, the candidate is a US Air Force Pararescueman. He is qualified to work with any Pararescue unit worldwide.

7. US Army Airborne School

This stage is also called jump school. Candidates learn basic **parachuting** skills.

9. Air Force Pararescue EMT-Paramedic Course

Training in emergency medical treatment and military evacuation procedures. Candidates work alongside paramedics and at local hospitals.

3 WEEKS

3 WEEKS

5 WEEKS

22 WEEKS

24 WEEKS

6. US Air Force Basic Survival School

Training in how to survive with few supplies in remote areas.

8. US Army Military Free-Fall Parachutist Course

Training in free-fall parachuting. Each candidate makes at least 30 free-fall jumps.

10. Air Force Pararescue Recovery Specialist Course

Training includes field medical care and **tactics**, mountaineering, combat tactics, advanced parachuting, and **insertion** and **extraction** by **helicopter**.

CHAPTER 7

TRADITIONS

When a candidate graduates from pipeline training, he is awarded a maroon **beret**. The beret has a pin called the Pararescue flash. The flash shows a guardian angel with its arms wrapped around the world. The words "That Others May Live" appear on the flash. The beret and flash are very important to a PJ. They represent hard work, **dedication**, heart, and soul.

There is a special **ritual** for when a PJ dies or is killed in action. His fellow PJs march one by one to the casket. At the casket, each man salutes, removes his **beret**, and takes off the flash. He puts his flash in the casket. The soldier is buried with all the flashes of his fellow PJs.

During the **Vietnam War**, another tradition began. An unofficial emblem of the Pararescue Jumpers is a pair of green footprints. They represent the Sikorsky HH-3E **helicopter** used during the war. The helicopter was huge and green. It was nicknamed "the Jolly Green Giant." Some people who were rescued by PJs got green footprints **tattooed** on their buttocks. The tattoos represented the PJs saving their butts.

When not on a mission, PJs proudly wear their maroon berets.

CHAPTER 8

VEHICLES

& GEAR

PJ VEHICLES

Pararescue Jumpers arrive in war zones and **disaster** areas in different ways. They often **parachute** in from **helicopters** or airplanes. Depending on the rescue plan, they might land on the ground or in the water. Once they land, they might need to use snowmobiles, all-**terrain** vehicles, rafts, or jet skis.

HC-130P Combat King aircraft

HH-60
Pave Hawk
helicopter

Zodiac inflatable boat

PJ GEAR

If the drop is from a high altitude, the PJ will have an oxygen mask. If the landing zone is in the water, the PJ will have SCUBA equipment. He will also carry medical supplies, survival gear, and a variety of weapons. Different missions require different gear. All together, a PJ might wear and carry as much as 170 pounds (77 kg).

Water Rescue Gear

tactical compass

scuba vest

swim fins

Air Rescue Gear

parachute helmet

altimeter

Mountain Rescue Gear

ice picks

climbing harness & gloves

crampons

snowshoes

Combat Rescue Gear

tactical vest

assault rifle

ballistic helmet & goggles

night vision goggles

CHAPTER 9

THE MOST
DECORATED
PJ

A regular part of a PJ's job is to risk his life to rescue someone. Sometimes the rescue mission is especially dangerous. A PJ who has performed above and beyond his duties earns an award. It includes a special badge for his uniform. The expression "highly decorated" means a soldier has earned several awards.

The most highly decorated Pararescueman is Chief Master Sergeant

Hackney was a Senior Airman when he received the Air Force Cross.

Duane Hackney. Hackney graduated at the top of his Pararescue class and served in the **Vietnam War**. On February 6, 1967, Hackney was on a typical rescue mission. His team found a pilot who had been seriously injured in a plane crash. Hackney got the pilot aboard the rescue **helicopter**. As the helicopter took off, it was hit by enemy fire.

Hackney when he was a Technical Sergeant

Hackney put his own **parachute** on the wounded pilot. He pushed him out the door. Hackney found another parachute just as the helicopter was hit again. The explosion threw him out the door. He was able to pull the cord to open the chute. However, he didn't have time to put the parachute on properly. He had to just hold on to it.

Even though he was wounded and badly burned, Hackney wasn't captured. A fellow PJ rescued him. For giving up his parachute and risking his own life, he received the Air Force Cross.

Over his career, Hackney earned more than 70 individual awards for heroic action. Hackney retired in 1991. He died in 1993. In June 2006, the US Air Force gave him one more honor. The Training facility at Lackland Air Force Base in San Antonio, Texas, was renamed the Hackney Training Complex.

CHAPTER 10

THE FUTURE OF THE
PARARESCUE
JUMPERS

Pararescue Jumpers are active all over the world. PJs supported United Nations troops in Somalia and Kosovo. In 1989, they saved hundreds of lives after California's Loma Prieta earthquake. They came to the rescue of mountaineers stuck on Alaska's Mount McKinley in 2011.

In Afghanistan and Iraq, PJs provide rescue services to United States and **coalition** forces. Since the 9/11 attacks in 2001, PJs have saved more than 12,000 soldiers' lives. Over that same time, they have saved more than 5,000 **civilian** lives.

PJs prepare to parachute into the Pacific Ocean to rescue injured sailors on a fishing boat.

The PJs are on alert 24 hours a day. When the need is there, they are ready to step into action immediately. This might mean going deep into a combat zone to rescue a downed pilot, or helping victims of **terrorism**. Or saving **civilians** injured or trapped by a natural **disaster**. Whatever the challenge, the PJs are always ready to do their best so that others may live.

TIMELINE

1943
Medics parachute into a remote area of Burma to rescue 20 people.

1967
Hackney performs above and beyond his duties and earns the Air Force Cross.

2011
Pararescue Jumpers rescue injured mountaineers stranded on Mount McKinley.

1940
Steerable parachutes are used by the government for the first time.

1947
Air Force Pararescue is created.

1989
Pararescue Jumpers help after an earthquake in and around San Francisco, California.

2005
Hurricane Katrina sweeps through New Orleans. PJs arrive on the scene and rescue thousands of people.